A Tasty Rainbow

By Adriana Diaz-Donoso
Illustrated by Rea Diwata Mendoza

Library For All Ltd.

Library For All is an Australian not for profit organisation with a mission to make knowledge accessible to all via an innovative digital library solution. Visit us at libraryforall.org

A Tasty Rainbow

This edition published 2022

Published by Library For All Ltd
Email: info@libraryforall.org
URL: libraryforall.org

Library For All gratefully acknowledges the contributions of all who made previous editions of this book possible.

Original illustrations by Rea Diwata Mendoza

A Tasty Rainbow
Diaz-Donoso, Adriana
ISBN: 978-1-922827-24-1
SKU02658

A Tasty Rainbow

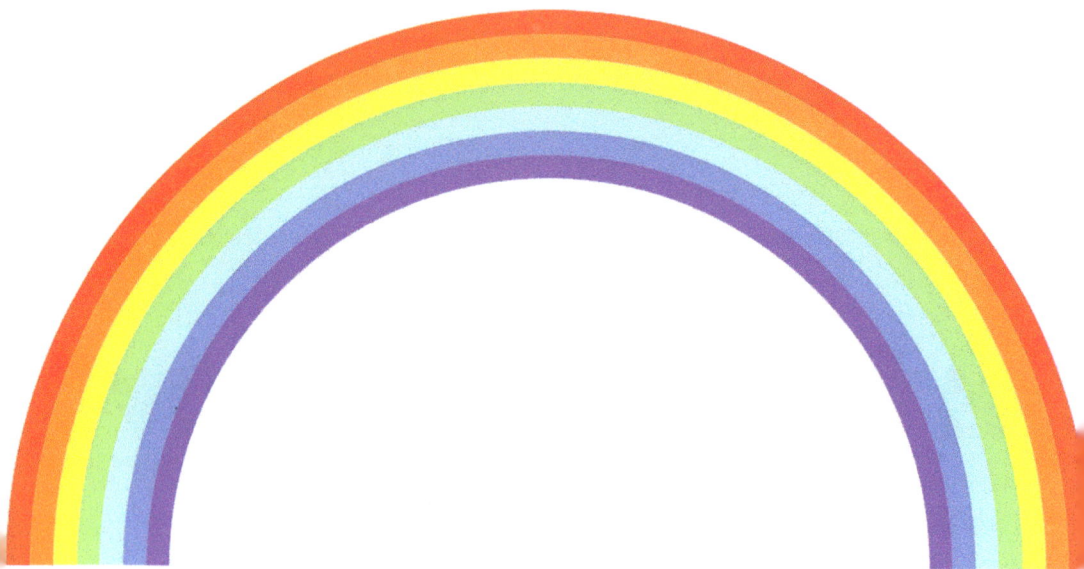

Did you know that in the land of fruits and vegetables, there are as many colours as the rainbow?

A banana is yellow, soft, and very sweet.

Some apples are red and juicy.

Do you know other colours of apples?

An orange is orange.

It is also very juicy
and sweet.

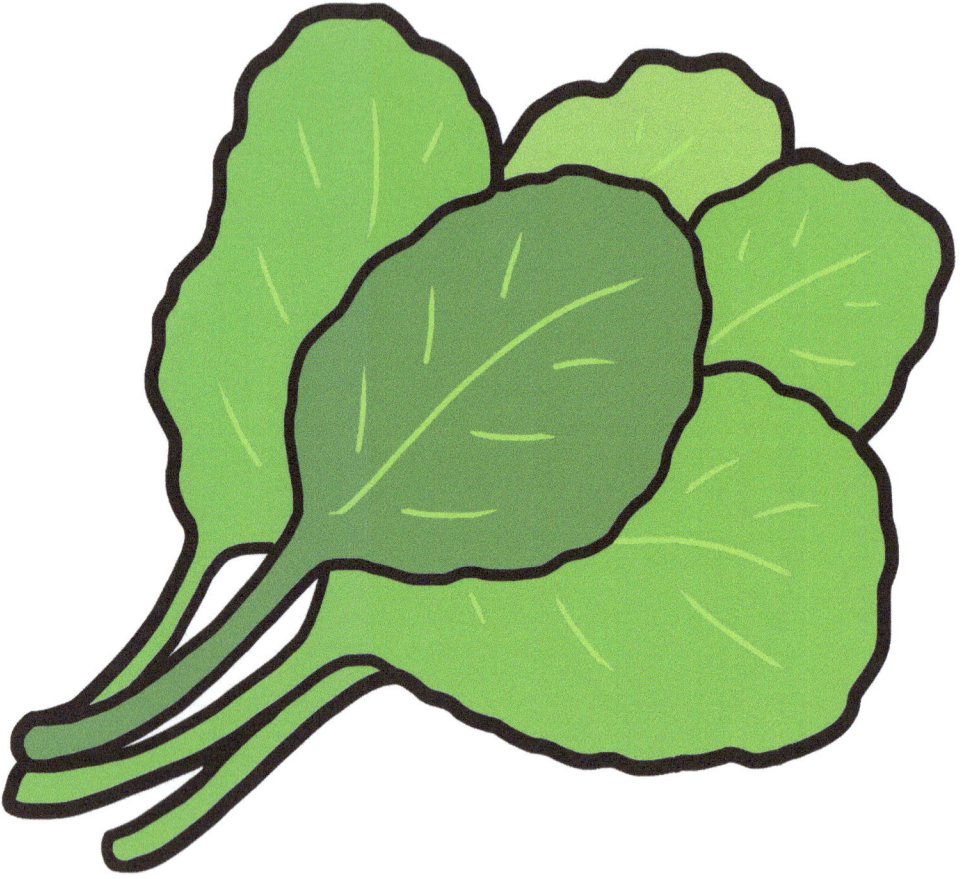

10

Spinach is green, and you can eat it fresh or cooked.

Blueberries are blue, and you can eat them fresh or in a delicious jam.

Eggplants are purple, and usually people cook them before eating.

Fruits and vegetables have different colours.

We need to eat all these colours because each of them has special vitamins that protect us against diseases.

As you see, in the land of fruits and vegetables, there are beautiful colours and many tastes.

They also give us energy to play and go to school.

So do not forget to have a colourful rainbow on your plate every day!

You can use these questions to talk about this book with your family, friends and teachers.

What did you learn from this book?

Describe this book in one word. Funny? Scary? Colourful? Interesting?

How did this book make you feel when you finished reading it?

What was your favourite part of this book?

download our reader app
getlibraryforall.org

About the contributors

Library For All works with authors and illustrators from around the world to develop diverse, relevant, high quality stories for young readers. Visit libraryforall.org for the latest news on writers' workshop events, submission guidelines and other creative opportunities.

Did you enjoy this book?

We have hundreds more expertly curated original stories to choose from.

We work in partnership with authors, educators, cultural advisors, governments and NGOs to bring the joy of reading to children everywhere.

Did you know?

We create global impact in these fields by embracing the United Nations Sustainable Development Goals.

www.ingramcontent.com/pod-product-compliance
Lightning Source LLC
Chambersburg PA
CBHW040318050426
42452CB00018B/2907